**In My Backyard / En mi jardín**

# I SEE A SQUIRREL/
# PUEDO VER UNA ARDILLA

By Alex Appleby                    Traducción al español: Eduardo Alamán

**Gareth Stevens**
Publishing

Please visit our website, www.garethstevens.com. For a free color catalog of all our high-quality books, call toll free 1-800-542-2595 or fax 1-877-542-2596.

Library of Congress Cataloging-in-Publication Data

Appleby, Alex.
[I see a squirrel. English & Spanish]
I see a squirrel = Puedo ver una ardilla / Ryan Nagelhout.
    p. cm. — (In my backyard = En mi jardín)
ISBN 978-1-4339-8800-4 (library binding)
1. Squirrels—Juvenile literature. I. Title. II. Title: Puedo ver una ardilla.
QL737.R68N3418 2013
599.36—dc23
                                    2012026206

First Edition

Published in 2013 by
**Gareth Stevens Publishing**
111 East 14th Street, Suite 349
New York, NY 10003

Copyright © 2013 Gareth Stevens Publishing

Editor: Ryan Nagelhout
Designer: Katelyn Londino
Spanish Translation: Eduardo Alamán

Photo credits: Cover, pp. 1, 11 iStockphoto/Thinkstock.com; p. 5 Bill Mack/Shutterstock.com; p. 7 aspen rock/Shutterstock.com; p. 9 Hemera/Thinkstock.com; pp. 13, 24 (teeth) John Czenke/Shutterstock.com; p. 15 James M Phelps, Jr/Shutterstock.com; p. 17 HGalina/Shutterstock.com; pp. 19, 24 (dens) ©iStockphoto.com/lilly3; p. 21 USBFCO/Shutterstock.com; p. 23 Nicholas Jr/Photo Researchers/Getty Images; p. 24 (seeds) Comstock/Thinkstock.com.

Printed in the United States of America

CPSIA compliance information: Batch #CW13GS: For further information contact Gareth Stevens, New York, New York at 1-800-542-2595.

# Contents

# Contenido

A squirrel is
a small rodent.

----------------------------------------

Las ardillas son
roedores pequeños.

It has a long, furry tail.
It is very soft.

---------------------------------

Las ardillas tienen una
cola larga y peluda.
La cola es muy suave.

It moves very fast.

-------------------------------

Las ardillas se mueven
muy rápido.

It runs away
from any danger.

------------------------------------

Se escapan de
cualquier peligro.

It has four big front teeth. They never stop growing!

------------------------------

Las ardillas tienen cuatro dientes grandes. ¡Los dientes no dejan de crecer!

13

Big teeth help
squirrels eat.

---

Los dientes las ayudan
a comer.

It eats nuts, plants, and seeds.

-------------------------------------------

Las ardillas comen nueces, plantas y semillas.

A ground squirrel digs
holes to live in.
These are called dens.

-----------------------------------

Las ardillas de tierra
cavan hoyos para vivir.
A estos se les llama
madrigueras.

A tree squirrel hops from tree to tree. It likes to eat tree sap!

---

Las ardillas trepadoras brincan de un árbol a otro. ¡Les gusta comer la savia!

A flying squirrel lives in trees! It can jump over 150 feet!

---

¡Las ardillas voladoras viven en árboles! ¡Pueden brincar hasta 150 pies!

23

# Words to Know/
# Palabras que debes saber

den/
(la) madriguera

seeds/
(las) semillas

teeth/
(los) dientes

# Index / Índice